Tuesday Shannon

THE ROUGH GUIDE TO ILKESTON

Rack Press

First published in in a limited edition of 150 copies,
the first fifty numbered and signed by the author.

Some of these poems, or earlier versions of them, have previously appeared in *PN Review*, *Wild Court*, *Take Three (Soundswrite Press*, 2019) and *LeftLion*. For their love, support, and encouragement I would like to thank the following people: Susan and Kian Williams, Paris and Chris Fletcher, Róisín King, Rory Waterman.

For Tez
We miss you, Pops.

Published in Wales by Rack Press,
The Old Manse, Broad Street, Presteigne, Powys, LD8 2AD

All orders and correspondence: rackpress@nicholasmurray.co.uk

ISBN 978-1-8382303-8-8

Printed by Artisan Print, Presteigne, Powys

Wentworth Street

A fat mallard slices through the canal,
its heft creasing the plate-glass surface
in a rippling ‘v’, like a hand
sweeping a freshly made bed.

In the blood-orange dawn,
the fur of evening frost along the footpath
flickers, and beyond the thin veil of trees
the morning traffic wheezes
its television-static breath.

And in black aerosol across the red-brick bridge:
ROAD TO NOWHERE.

'HOPE'

Between a boarded-up chippy
and a boarded-up florist
second- or third- hand
refrigerators lean to attention.

But there are no passers-by
no eyes to catch and tempt –
just fallen leaves, empty buses,
artificial light.

In the shelter of the closed shop doorway
a teenager tugs at his hoodie,
lifts a cigarette with his left hand,
shakes a canister in his right.

Across every shutter
one word in thick black paint
repeats like a mantra, or prayer.
The streetlights flicker on.

Dredging

When they dragged the carcass
from the canal-bed, thirty years of rust
had made it impossible to tell

that once it was the red of the heavy summer strawberries
your grandmother's arthritic hands twisted from the vine
to stir into jam, or sneak to your waiting mouth.

Its saddle had once smelled of new leather,
like the armchair she'd hoisted herself from
when she heard you ringing that once silver bell.

Every day of that heatwave it carried you
from your door to hers, where tea and buttered toast
always awaited you, somehow.

Now the spokes of its wheels,
long stripped of inner-tube and tyre,
sink back into silt, into memory.

Bennerley Viaduct

There was a faint rattling noise. Away to the right, the train, like a luminous caterpillar, was threading across the night. The rattling ceased. "She's over the viaduct. You'll just do it."
D.H. Lawrence, Sons and Lovers, *1913*

Lawrence wrote about how the train zipped
along the seam where the two counties are stitched together,
steam engines rattling over the valley,
carts carrying coal to the south.
The Luftwaffe tried to flatten it; Heinkels
released their bombs and missed their mark.
So we take a picnic, walk the footpath that runs where tracks
ran,
eat sandwiches in silence, staring at a timeless
uneven green. Beneath us, the Erewash twists its way
toward the Trent.

The Flowers

are dying.

Mum has moved over to his side of the bed
and we take turns to climb
in beside her –
hopeful that grief
won't steal the air from her
like on the first night.

People bring more flowers.

From his bedroom my brother
texts me, knowing there are more people
in the kitchen than he can face
so I make tea and toast and sneak away.

We've run out of vases.

One sister can't stay in the house,
the other can't leave it.
There's too much to do and we don't know
how to do it and we need
butter and bread and milk and cheese
but people bring flowers
and there's nowhere to put them so the flowers
are dying, Dad is dead, and I'm making coffee.

Catechism

In the vestibule, Mum dips her hand in holy water,
blesses each of her wayward flock
with the sign of the cross.

We are well-practised in this deception:
know when to kneel, stand, and pray,
say 'amen' in the right places and,

at the call for Communion, remain seated.
Before this grief, I would've grinned
at our perfectly-timed performances,

not understanding the comforts
of polished pews,
polished answers.

The Regulars

i.

9:55, he paces as he waits for the bar
to be lifted from the heavy wooden door,
and filters in with the usual Thursday morning pension crowd.
After their orders of coffee, toast, seniors' breakfasts,
he asks for his drink in a tall glass, no ice –

and I am reminded of being fifteen,
refilling Dad's Smirnoff
to hide at the back of the cupboard.

His voice shows no trace of this town,
no drawn-out Midlands vowels, as he tells me
about a job interview in the city,
how he's having a few to settle his nerves.

The same lie he's told me seven times this year.
Another one for the road.

He hands back his glass and I pour again
because I am paid to oblige, nothing more.

Then he asks about me, and because I am paid to oblige
I tell him I'm working my way through university.

My son did the same, he replies,
though they've long been estranged.

One more. He smiles, and again I pour.
He downs in a gulp, then makes for the door.
Good luck! I call, but he's forgotten his lie,
he'll be back next Thursday, pension day, same time.

ii.

His fist is as soft as a block
of butter, shaking
around two pound coins
and a twenty pence piece,
to be exchanged
for the first pint of the day.

Under the tap it pours
itself, clouds, settles:
thick and brown with
a white halo the width
of forefinger and thumb.

His skin is the jaundiced shade
of pages in antique books,
and the ink of a decades-old tattoo
is blurred beyond comprehension

not that it matters
whether it reads Mother
or Martha, those who meant enough
to be honoured are long gone.

Nothing left but this
small pleasure, the glass
sweating as the tremors still.

iii.

Dying midsummer light
softens the creases and lines on skin
as sheer as bible-paper, dims the pallor
of the thick blue rivers confluent
and divergent across each limb.

He can almost pretend
he doesn't notice that each breath
is laboured, or that despite him cutting
her food into bite-sized chunks
she is eating less each day.

Each night the burden of lifting
her into bed is a little lighter,
a little heavier. Across the table
he clasps her hand, like a child
desperately holding his kite.

iv.

Outside, the church clock chimes eleven
and it echoes through the empty marketplace –
the stalls' steel skeletons set up,
glowing white in the stark LED light,
awaiting the morning's wares of knock-off
perfume and second-hand books.

When the bell rings for last orders
a small commotion ensues:
a rush for one more drink,
just another glass of wine.

The last pint poured and paid for,
I wipe down the bar, the tables, the menus,
collect the used glasses now full of fag-ends,
flat dregs, empty crisp packets.
Make idle conversation with my captors:

How's the kids?
How's work?
What's your mum up to these days?

Then I fill every fridge,
unscrew each nozzle to soak overnight,
sweep, mop, cash up,
bar the door, turn out the lights.